Who Has These Feet?

Laura Hulbert
illustrated by Erik Brooks

Henry Holt and Company · New York

Who
has
these feet?

A polar bear has these feet.

A polar bear has fur on the bottom
of its feet so it won't slip on the ice.

Who has these feet?

A tree frog has these feet.

A tree frog has sticky pads on its
toes so it can stick to leaves.

Who has these feet?

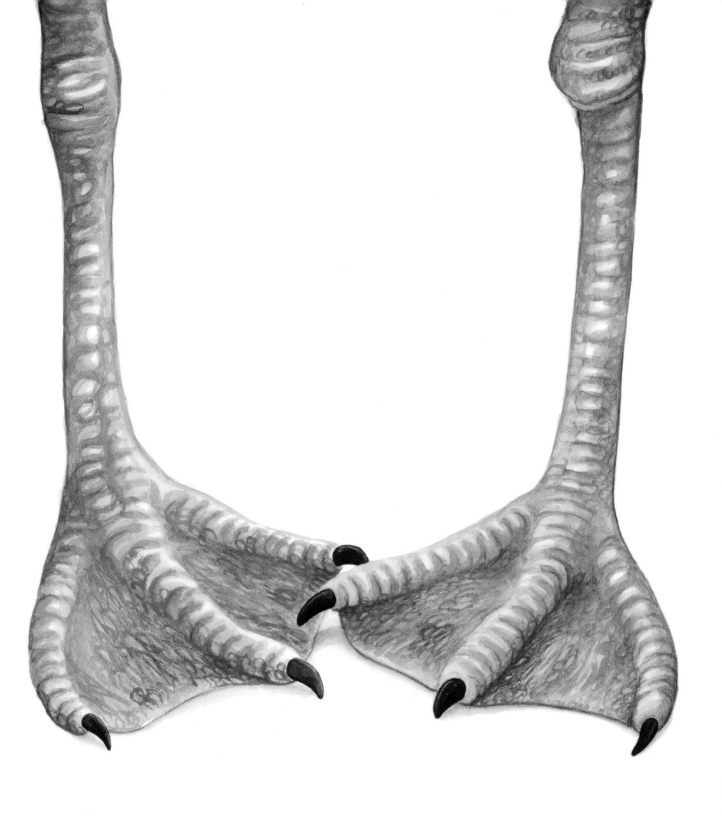

A duck has these feet.

A duck has webbed feet
so it can go fast in the water.

Who has these feet?

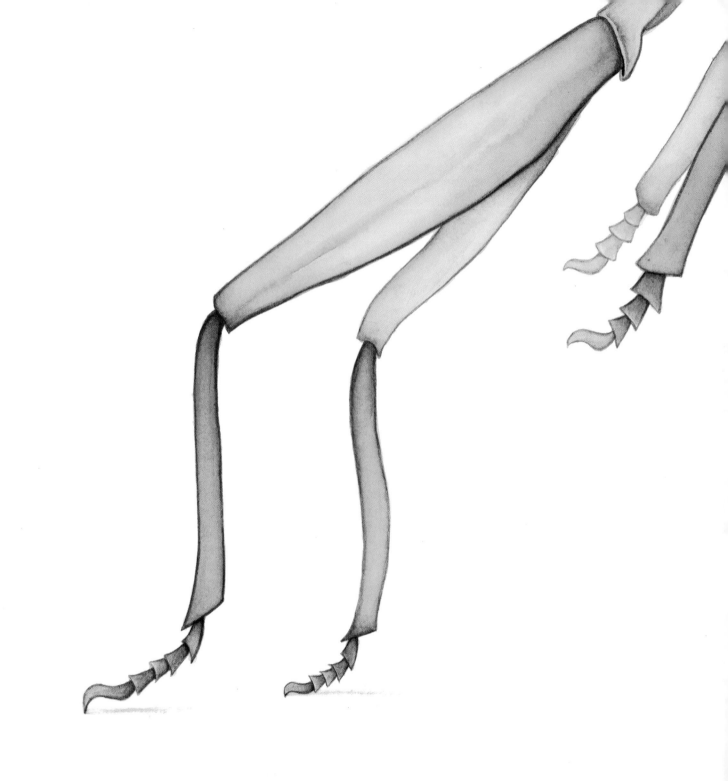

An ant has these feet.

An ant has claws on the end of its feet
so it can dig a nest under the ground.

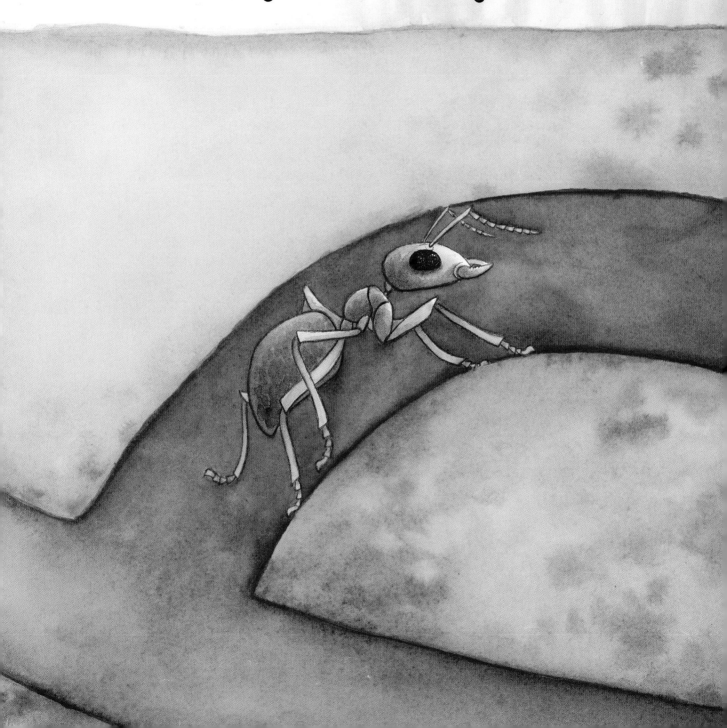

Who has these feet?

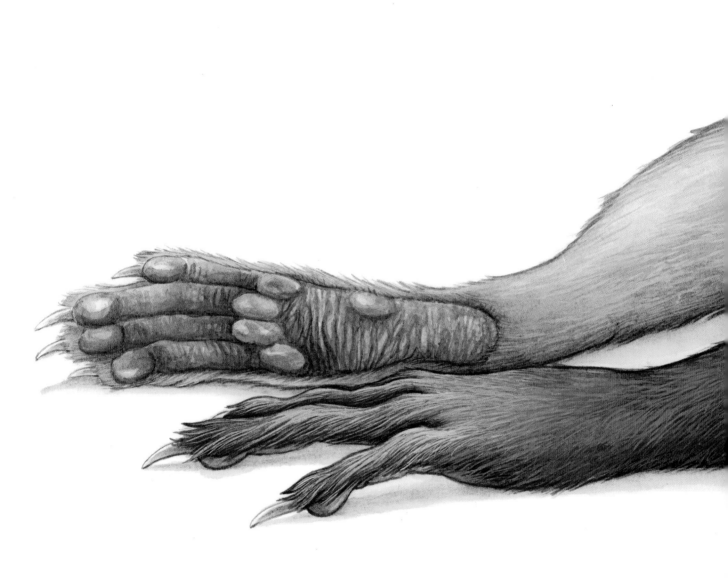

A squirrel has these feet.

A squirrel has claws on its toes
so it can run up and down trees.

Who has these feet?

A parrot has these feet.

A parrot has two toes in front and two toes in back so it can hold on to branches.

Who
has
these
feet?

A desert lizard has these feet.

A desert lizard has special scales around its toes
so it won't sink down into the sand.

Who
has
these
feet?

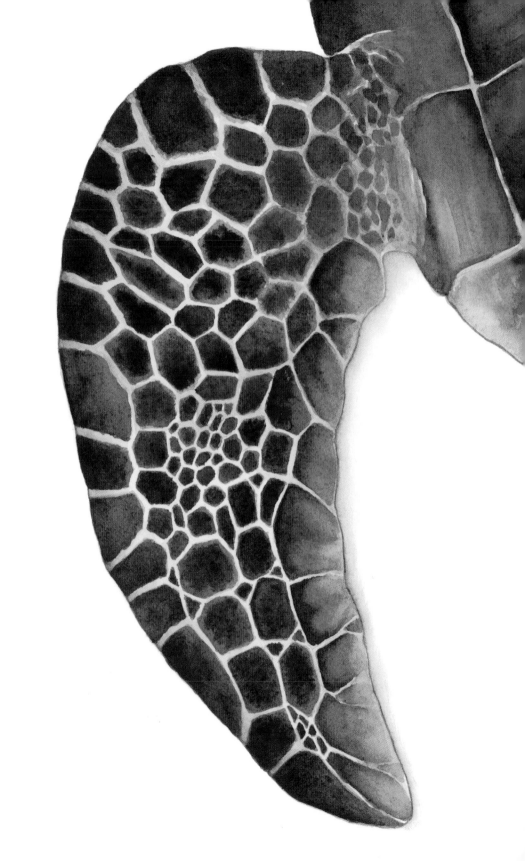

A sea turtle has these feet.

A sea turtle has flippers
so it can pull itself through the water.

Who has these feet?

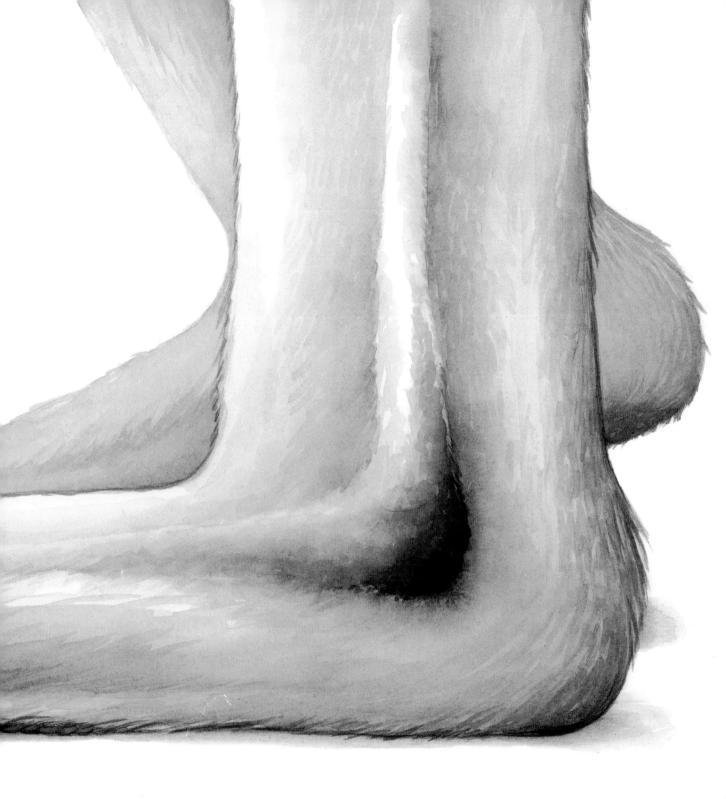

A kangaroo has these feet.

A kangaroo has big feet so it can hop for a long way as it looks for food.

We have

Who

has